Laying the Foundations
for Clean Development:
Preparing the Land Use Sector

A quick guide to the Clean Development Mechanism

Laying the Foundations for Clean Development: Preparing the Land Use Sector

A quick guide to the Clean Development Mechanism

Louise Aukland and Pedro Moura Costa, from EcoSecurities;
Stephen Bass, Saleemul Huq, and Natasha Landell-Mills, from IIED;
Richard Tipper and Rebecca Carr, from The Edinburgh Centre for
Carbon Management

Laying the Foundations for Clean Development: Preparing the Land Use Sector

A quick guide to the Clean Development Mechanism

This publication is an output from a research project funded by the United Kingdom Department for International Development (DFID) for the benefit of developing countries. The views expressed are not necessarily those of the UK Government.

DFID Forestry Research Programme ZF0167
March 2002

Website: www.cdmcapacity.org

Citation: Aukland L, Moura Costa P, Bass S, Huq S, Landell-Mills N, Tipper R, and Carr R, 2002. Laying the Foundations for Clean Development: Preparing the Land Use Sector. A quick guide to the Clean Development Mechanism. IIED, London.

Designed by: My Word!, 138 Railway Terrace, Rugby CV21 3HN

Printed by: The Russell Press Ltd, Nottingham, NG6 0BT

Preface

Many people working in land use and forestry are becoming increasingly aware of the inclusion of their sector in international policy discussions about climate change. Rising levels of atmospheric carbon are a major cause of global climate change. Land-based ecosystems play important roles here, both positively by acting as a 'sink' for carbon (sequestering carbon through photosynthesis), and negatively as a 'source' of carbon (through deforestation, decomposition, soil erosion, etc).

Of particular importance to developing countries is the emergence of new opportunities for developing, and attracting foreign investment into, carbon mitigation projects. For the land-use sector, this includes afforestation and reforestation. These opportunities are provided within the context of the Clean Development Mechanism (CDM) of the Kyoto Protocol, the international agreement on climate change.

This booklet provides information to forestry and land-use audiences, principally in developing countries, who want to find out more about the CDM and how it affects their activities. It introduces the existing policy and regulatory framework of the CDM. It offers guidance on the eligibility of different project activities. It lays out what countries can do to prepare for CDM in the land-use sector. And it looks to the future, providing insight into the wider implications and future developments of the CDM.

Contents

1. What is the Clean Development Mechanism?

What is the Climate Change Convention?

This is a United Nations agreement to stabilise greenhouse gases in the atmosphere, at a level that would prevent dangerous changes to the climate. The Convention on Climate Change was agreed at the United Nations Conference on Environment and Development (UNCED) in Rio, 1992. To date, 186 countries have ratified the convention.

To put the convention into operation, a protocol was outlined in Kyoto in 1997. The most important aspect of the Kyoto Protocol is its legally binding commitments for 39 developed countries to reduce their greenhouse gas (GHG) emissions by an average of 5.2% relative to 1990 levels. These emission reductions must be achieved by 2008–2012: the so called '**first commitment period**'. The developed countries with emission reduction targets are called the **Annex 1** countries, whereas those without targets are the **non-Annex 1** countries (see Glossary for definitions).

The Kyoto Protocol allows developed countries to reach their targets in different ways through '**Flexibility Mechanisms**'. These include: Emissions Trading (trading of emission allowances between developed nations); Joint Implementation (transferring emission allowances between developed nations, linked to specific emission-reduction projects); and the **Clean Development Mechanism (CDM)**. The CDM is the only Flexibility Mechanism that involves developing countries. It allows developed nations to achieve part of their reduction obligations through projects in developing countries that reduce emissions or 'fix' or sequester CO_2 from the atmosphere. This booklet describes the potential for land-use projects within the CDM. It provides guidance to people in developing countries who are responsible for establishing enabling policies and regulations in this area, as well as project developers.

How does the CDM affect developing countries?

At present, developing countries have no obligations to constrain their GHG emissions. But they are still able, on a voluntary basis, to contribute to global emission reductions by hosting projects under the Clean Development Mechanism.

The CDM has two key goals:

- To assist developing countries who host CDM projects to achieve sustainable development;

■ To provide developed countries with flexibility for achieving their emission reduction targets, by allowing them to take credits from emission reducing projects undertaken in developing countries.

The greenhouse gas benefits of each CDM project will be measured according to internationally agreed methods and will be quantified in standard units, to be known as **'Certified Emission Reductions'** (**CERs**). These are expressed in tons of CO_2 emission avoided. When the Kyoto Protocol becomes fully operational, it is anticipated that these 'carbon credits' will be bought and sold in a new environmental market; they are already becoming a commodity.

How is the CDM relevant to the land-use sector?

Rising atmospheric levels of CO_2 are the main driver of climate change. Figure 1 illustrates the global carbon budget. The boxes show the stocks of carbon held in different parts of the earth and atmosphere. The arrows indicate the annual flows of carbon between the main components. The largest flows between oceans, forests and the atmosphere occur naturally. But emissions from burning fossil fuels and producing cement upset the natural balance and increase CO_2 in the atmosphere – leading to climate instability. People's impacts on forests and soils are also a key factor, with almost 25% of annual emissions of CO_2 resulting from forest clearance. However, tree planting or regeneration of forest ecosystems removes CO_2 from the atmosphere as vegetation grows; a process referred to as 'carbon sequestration'. (Around 50% of the dry weight of woody vegetation is

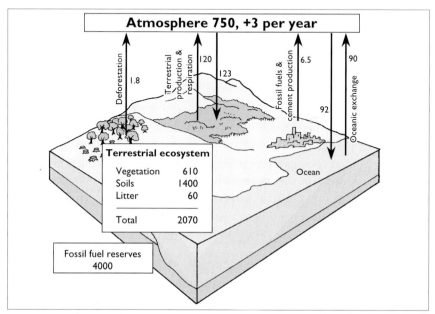

Figure 1: Carbon stocks are presented in Gt and carbon Gty^{-1}

> ### Box 1: How did the current rules evolve?
>
> The role of land use, land use change and forestry (or 'LULUCF' or 'sinks' in negotiators' jargon) in the Climate Change Convention has undergone a complex evolution. The Kyoto Protocol refers to two main groups of activities: afforestation, reforestation and deforestation (or ARD, Article 3.3): and additional human-induced activities for the agricultural and forestry sectors not included in ARD (Article 3.4). However, Article 12 on the CDM referred only to 'emission reductions' with no mention of any specific activities. This led to a variety of interpretations as to the possible role of land use and forestry in the CDM.
>
> Land use and forestry rapidly became a hot topic for the meetings of the Conference of Parties (CoP). At the 4th CoP, in 1998, a target date of 2000 was set for decisions relating to the use of land use and forestry, or 'sinks'. At the 6th CoP in 2000, opposing views on the inclusion of forestry activities within the CDM contributed to the collapse of negotiations.
>
> After the withdrawal of the United States from the Kyoto process in March 2001, there was a renewed urgency to salvage something from the failed 6th CoP. At the resumed meeting, held in July 2001, decisions were eventually made on sinks in the CDM. Afforestation and reforestation are the only eligible land use activities for the first commitment period (2008–2012). A limit was also put on the use of land use based CDM projects towards Annex-1 emission reduction targets. Only 1% of a developed country's base year emissions, for each year of the 5-year commitment period, can be achieved using sinks. This is equivalent to about 20% of the country's target. The role of land use and forestry projects in the CDM beyond 2012 will be decided as part of the negotiations on the second commitment period.
>
> The 7th CoP held in Marrakech in November 2001, appointed a CDM Executive Board (10 members), which is establishing more detailed rules and guidance for projects, including for land use projects.

carbon.) Soil management is also key, as soils contain substantially more carbon than is contained in the atmosphere. Different land use activities will therefore have different impacts on the carbon balance: some may result in net sequestration and others in net emissions.

The role of forestry in meeting the objectives of the Climate Change Convention has been contentious throughout the negotiations. Although it is recognised that land use is integral to the carbon cycle, there is a diversity of opinion on its exact role in meeting emission-reduction targets (see Box 1). A decision was made in Bonn, in July 2001, to include afforestation and reforestation as the only eligible land-use activities in the CDM. These may be large or small-scale, single or multiple species, pure forestry or on farm systems (illustrated in Figure 2), such as:

- Establishment of woodlots on communal lands.
- Reforestation of marginal areas with native species, e.g. riverine areas, steep slopes, around and between existing forest fragments (through planting and natural regeneration).

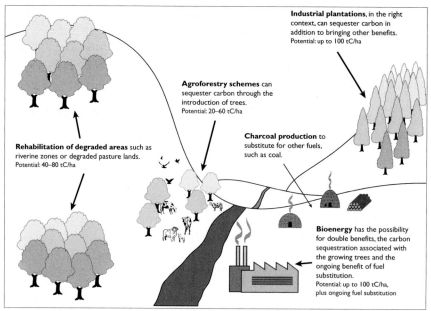

Figure 2: Eligible land use activites in the CDM. With an estimate for their potential for generating carbon offsets (In tonnes of carbon per hectare, tC/ha)

- New, large-scale, industrial plantations.
- Establishment of biomass plantations for energy production and the substitution of fossil fuels.
- Small-scale plantations by landowners.
- Introduction of trees into existing agricultural systems (agroforestry).
- Rehabilitation of degraded areas through tree planting or assisted natural regeneration.

What could I get out of the CDM?

Industrialised countries have gradually developed domestic policies to comply with the Kyoto Protocol. This has led to a growing demand for carbon credits. Developing countries may be well-placed to supply such carbon credits. While many factors influence the size and stability of the global market, some studies indicate that it could be in the order of billions of dollars a year. As a comparison, total foreign aid for forestry activities in developing countries amounts to about US$ 1.5 billion a year.

The impact that the CDM will have on developing-country stakeholders will vary, depending on: the objectives and priorities of those stakeholders; the planning and regulation in place to ensure that projects address these objectives and priorities; and the current land use and organisational framework upon which CDM projects will be built. CDM can offer developing-country governments the opportunity to promote and attract investment in sustainable forestry, land restoration, energy efficiency and renewable-energy projects. For a project developer, it may offer the additional input required to make a project financially viable. For a local farmer, it may provide an additional source of income, or access to technical support.

The ways in which the CDM rules and procedures evolve will depend on numerous factors, many of which can still be influenced by developing-country stakeholders. However, if the process of developing and regulating CDM projects is not properly planned, some of these potential opportunities may not materialise, or may even turn into problems. Section 2 addresses how developing countries can prepare for the CDM and ensure that the needs of the land-use sector are addressed. Section 3 discusses potential pitfalls of unplanned development of the CDM in developing countries.

What are the CDM rules and conditions?

CDM projects need to seek approval by the CDM Executive Board. A number of rules and conditions will apply, some to all project types, and others specifically to afforestation and reforestation projects. While several of the detailed procedures to be applied to CDM forestry projects are still to be agreed, the overall framework is already established for approving projects and accounting for the carbon credits generated:

1. Only areas that were not forest on 31st December 1989 are likely to meet the CDM definitions of afforestation or reforestation.
2. Projects must result in real, measurable and long-term emission reductions, as certified by a third-party agency (**'operational entities'** in the language of the convention). The carbon stocks generated by the project need to be secure over the long term (a point referred to as **'permanence'**), and any future emissions that might arise from these stocks need to be accounted for.
3. Emission reductions or sequestration must be **additional** to any that would occur without the project. They must result in a net storage of carbon and therefore a net removal of carbon dioxide from the atmosphere. This is called **'additionality'** and is assessed by comparing the carbon stocks and flows of the project activities with those that would have occurred without the project (its **'baseline'**). For example, the project may be proposing to afforest farmland with native tree species, increasing its stocks of carbon. By comparing the carbon stored in the 'project' plantations (high carbon) with the carbon that would have been stored in the 'baseline' abandoned farmland (low carbon) it is possible to calculate the net carbon benefit. There are still a number of technical discussions regarding the interpretation of the 'additionality' requirement for specific contexts.

4. Projects must be in line with **sustainable development objectives,** as defined by the government that is hosting them.
5. Projects must contribute to biodiversity conservation and sustainable use of natural resources.
6. Only projects starting from the year 2000 onwards will be eligible.
7. Two percent of the carbon credits awarded to a CDM project will be allocated to a fund to help cover the costs of adaptation in countries severely affected by climate change (the '**adaptation levy**'). This adaptation fund may provide support for land use activities that are not presently eligible under the CDM, for example conservation of existing forest resources.
8. Some of the proceeds from carbon credit sales from all CDM projects will be used to cover administrative expenses of the CDM (a proportion still to be decided).
9. Projects need to select a crediting period for activities, either a maximum of seven years that can be renewed at most two times, or a maximum of ten years with no renewal option.
10. The funding for CDM projects must not come from a diversion of official development assistance (ODA) funds.
11. Each CDM project's management plan must address and account for potential **leakage.** Leakage is the unplanned, indirect emissions of CO_2, resulting from the project activities. For example, if the project involves the establishment of plantations on agricultural land, then leakage could occur if people who were farming on this land migrated to clear forest elsewhere.

What is covered by the definitions of 'afforestation' and 'reforestation'?

Although afforestation and reforestation are the only eligible land-use activities in the CDM, there is some uncertainty over which definitions will be adopted. This is currently under review, with a decision expected at the 9th CoP in 2003. The definitions in the official negotiating text, as of 2002, relate to Articles 3.3 and 3.4 of the Protocol (forest and land-use activities within developed countries):

■ 'Afforestation' is the direct human-induced conversion of land that has not been forested for a period of at least 50 years to forested land through planting, seeding and/or the human-induced promotion of natural seed sources.
■ 'Reforestation' is the direct human-induced conversion of non-forested land to forested land through planting, seeding or human-induced promotion of natural seed sources, on land that was forested but that has been converted to non-forested land. For the first commitment

period (2008–2012), reforestation activities will be limited to reforestation occurring on those lands that did not contain forest on 31st December 1989.

■ 'Forest' is a minimum area of land of 0.05–1.0 hectares with tree crown cover of more than 10–30 per cent with trees, with the potential to reach a minimum height of 2–5 metres at maturity in situ. A forest may consist either of closed forest formations, where trees of various storeys and undergrowth cover a high proportion of the ground or open forest. Young natural stands and all plantations which have yet to reach a crown density of 10–30 per cent or tree height of 2–5 metres are included under forest, as are areas normally forming part of the forest area which are temporarily unstocked as a result of human intervention such as harvesting or natural causes but which are expected to revert to forest.

Even if these definitions are applied to the CDM, it is likely that developing-country governments will have to decide what definitions best apply to their natural ecosystems, within the scope of the definitions quoted here. The strict application of these definitions to CDM, however, would exclude any forest rehabilitation, revegetation, enrichment planting and natural regeneration-type projects that did not involve the conversion of 'non-forest vegetation' to 'forest vegetation'. This would restrict the scope and possible benefits arising from CDM land-use projects (see Box 2).

What other CDM rules remain to be decided?
Many CDM rules and conditions for land-use projects still remain to be agreed. These include approaches for:

■ calculating the net carbon benefit of CDM projects;
■ dealing with flexible and non-permanent land-use systems;
■ addressing the social and environmental impacts of projects.

Although decisions will be made at international level, their impact on the ground and for projects will be significant. Two advisory groups to the Climate Convention, called the Subsidiary Body for Scientific and Technological Advice (**SBSTA**) and the Intergovernmental Panel on Climate Change (**IPCC**), will be preparing advice and guidance for a series of meetings between now and the 9th CoP (due in 2003). Developing country agencies are still able to contribute to this process, via their National Focal Points or by sending delegations to attend the IPCC and SBSTA meetings. In the meantime, projects can already be developed using existing methodologies, subject to adjustments once final rules are defined. There is also a range of activities that developing countries can do to

Box 2: Rehabilitating degraded areas: Face Foundation in Malaysia

The Innoprise-FACE Foundation Rainforest Rehabilitation Project (INFAPRO) This was the first large-scale forestry-based carbon offset project in the world. Its objective is to rehabilitate 25,000 ha of degraded areas by enrichment planting and forest reclamation, using indigenous tree species such as dipterocarps, fast growing pioneers, and forest fruit trees. It is a co-operative venture between the Sabah Foundation, a semi-government forestry organisation in the state of Sabah, Malaysia, and the FACE Foundation of the Netherlands. The total investment committed by the FACE Foundation amounts to US\$ 15 million. It is expected that the project will sequester at least 4.25 million tonnes of carbon (15.6 million tonnes CO_2) during its lifetime at an average cost of US\$ 3.52 per ton of carbon (US\$ 0.95 per t CO_2).

The planting phase will last for 25 years and the forests will be maintained for 99 years. The long-term nature of the project should enable the maintenance and silvicultural treatments required to sustain growth rates during the project's life. It is expected that at the end of the first 60-year growth cycle, these forests will be exploited for timber, which belongs to the Sabah Foundation. However, timber harvesting will have to be done in a careful way, so that a healthy residual stand can again regenerate a well-stocked forest in order to maintain a carbon pool for the FACE Foundation, which has the exclusive rights to the carbon sequestered through the 99 years of the project.

As well as sequestered carbon, the project will produce over 4 million m³ of sawn hardwood timber over the project lifetime. As the Foundation is a semi-government organisation with the mandate of improving people's welfare in the state of Sabah, it is expected that the project will also generate considerable social benefits: it is expected to generate 230 jobs per year in the planting phase, as well as substantial research and training of Malaysian students.

This case study illustrates how the Kyoto Protocol's definitions of forestry could affect the eligibility of projects. If the current definition of afforestation and reforestation used for activities in developed countries is strictly applied, this project may not be eligible under the Kyoto Protocol, since the areas to be rehabilitated have a dense canopy cover and would already be classed as 'forest'. Appropriate definitions of forestry would have to be adopted to enable the inclusion of a wider range of projects.

Box 3: What will happen with existing 'Activities Implemented Jointly' pilot projects?

As a learning exercise, an Activities Implemented Jointly (AIJ) pilot phase was established in 1994, whereby projects would be established in order to gain experiences – but without any formal carbon crediting allowed between developed and developing countries. Despite plans to have the CDM in place by 2000, this was not achieved and the pilot phase continues. It is unclear what will happen to existing AIJ projects once the CDM is fully operational and whether or not they will be transferable to the CDM.

prepare and facilitate the development of CDM projects. Section 2 explores some of these.

2. How can we prepare for the CDM?

The success of CDM projects in developing countries will depend on the institutional and policy environment in which they operate. Relevant policies include those on forestry, planning, sustainable development, rural land use, and poverty alleviation. This section will address how developing countries can prepare for the CDM by creating an environment that will encourage appropriate land-use projects.

What role can governments and planning agencies take?

The Kyoto Protocol ascribes the responsibility for determining the procedures for approving CDM projects to host countries (ie developing countries). Without such approval, projects cannot be submitted to the CDM Executive Board. Therefore developing country governments wishing to host CDM projects must set up these procedures.

Beyond simple approval or rejection of projects, there is much more that countries (and agencies within countries) can do to make CDM projects successful. These range from passive to pro-active, as follows:

- Setting up the minimum requirements for CDM projects, which could include meeting national sustainable development requirements, and the procedures for submitting projects for government approval;
- Producing a list of non-eligible activities (eg, some countries may wish to discourage certain land-use activities);
- Setting up an infrastructure for promoting and/or handling CDM projects, which could include a plan, identifying CDM priority areas and activities (preferably integrated with national land-use plans), extension services and support, provision of information about CDM opportunities, and investment facilitation;
- Developing a full programme to promote and actively seek out CDM projects. An example of this approach was the programme developed by the Costa Rican Office for Joint Implementation (OCIC), which provided advance finance for small-scale farmers to conduct forest management activities which would generate carbon credits that OCIC sold on the international market (see Box 4).

Those who wish to develop CDM projects may include land use or forest agencies in developing countries (or even NGOs or private sector actors). They need to be able to interact with the focal point in the government of the country concerned to find out what national-level procedures are in place. As few countries have put such procedures in place, land use and forestry agencies should assist the national government to develop relevant criteria.

What can be done to encourage appropriate CDM projects in the land-use sector?

Irrespective of host-government interest in the CDM, some requirements must be in place before a project can apply for registration with the CDM Executive Board. Other factors greatly support the implementation of the CDM, but are not themselves essential. Both essential and desirable institutional structures and enabling policies are outlined below:

Ratify the Kyoto Protocol

Participation in a CDM activity is possible only if the host country is party to the Kyoto Protocol. By February 2002, 47 parties had ratified the

---

Box 4: Government promoted programmes and direct payment to farmers: Costa Rica

In 1997, Costa Rica became the first developing country to launch a national carbon sequestration programme. The Private Forestry Programme (PFP) encourages land owners to opt for forestry-related land uses by providing direct payment for environmental services – CO_2 fixation, water quality, biodiversity, and landscape beauty. Monetary incentives aim to increase the attractiveness of forestry compared to environmentally damaging land uses. Incentives are paid to land owners over 5 years, following the signing of a contract to keep land under a specified use for at least 20 years. Farmers who sign up for these incentives, hand over their environmental service rights to the government, which in turn sells them to investors.

The institution co-ordinating these incentives is called FONAFIFO, a Forestry Financing Fund under the Ministry of Energy and Environment. FONAFIFO receives and analyses applications, conducts field verifications, carries out the payments, and monitors the forestry projects.

The carbon credits are marketed by the Costa Rican Office for Joint Implementation (OCIC). OCIC essentially acts as a 'one-stop-shop' for buying and selling carbon credits (known as Certified Tradable Offsets or CTOs). International investors interested in purchasing certified offsets go to OCIC, to purchase CTOs developed either by government programmes or by individual developers. Even where deals are negotiated bilaterally between buyers and sellers, they must be registered with OCIC. By centralising trading in carbon offsets, OCIC aims to lower transaction costs. The first batch of carbon credits (200,000 tons of carbon) was sold to a Norwegian consortium at US\$ 10/tC (US\$ 2.70/tCO$_2$), for a total of US\$ 2,000,000.

Beyond carbon credits, Costa Rica is also working on ways to commercialise other environmental services generated by forestry activities promoted by its programmes. One example is a system to charge hydroelectric plants for conserving their water catchments. A similar mechanism is being created for remunerating farmers in eco-tourism regions. In the case of biodiversity, genetic prospecting contracts have been signed between the Costa Rican institute of genetic resources and international pharmaceutical companies.

Protocol. However, projects initiated prior to ratification are likely to be allowed to be registered under the CDM after ratification.

Establish a National Authority for CDM

Countries need to designate a National Authority for the CDM in order to participate. This may, or may not, be the Focal Point for the Climate Convention. The National Authority should be situated so that it can effectively coordinate the agencies responsible for setting sustainability policies, environmental and investment regulations, and the organisations involved in CDM project development. It should provide:

- Clear guidelines on priority areas for projects, and on national project approval criteria;
- Efficient and transparent procedures for processing project applications;
- Procedures for registering and monitoring in-country project activities, including the assessment of local sustainability benefits and costs;
- Procedures for authorising verification organisations that validate and certify CDM projects;
- Clear guidelines on the selection, consultation and monitoring processes that are required of projects;
- Support in managing the risks associated with the national CDM portfolio, for example, by establishing reserve stocks of carbon credits that could be used as an insurance measure in the event of failure of certain projects;
- Information about project and financial opportunities to in-country project developers.

Develop sustainable development policies, plans and control systems

Clearly defined sustainable development objectives will greatly assist the development of CDM projects because developers and investors will be able to seek project opportunities that are consistent with these objectives (see box 5). Clear policies and control systems also make project planning and design much easier.

Develop and integrate national and regional policies

Countries that have policies in place on climate change issues, and specifically on the CDM, are more likely to be able to promote CDM projects that meet with broader national or regional objectives. The development of CDM projects in the land-use sector will be influenced by a number of policies, including those related to forestry and agriculture, land tenure, land-use planning, sustainable development, trade, investment, rural energy, etc. Better CDM projects may result if these

---

Box 5: Why is sustainable development important and what is it about?

Firstly, sustainable development is a requirement of the Kyoto Protocol. It is one of the CDM's two purposes: 'Assisting Parties not included in Annex I in achieving sustainable development' (Article 12). Secondly, a CDM project that aims at sustainable development will reduce its own environmental, social and political risk and improve its resilience. Finally, it is the host country's responsibility to specify the criteria for sustainable development.

Sustainable development means that the needs of the present generation are met without compromising the ability of future generations to meet their needs. Sustainable development entails integrating three objectives – environmental, social and economic. It is important not to make the mistake of treating sustainable development as an 'environmental' concern only – this can cause social or economic problems.

Balancing sustainability issues at different levels:

Project: e.g. how well soil and water are managed, how employees are being treated, impacts on neighbours' livelihoods and infrastructure provision, and other practical management issues. A key question: is the scheme using best locally appropriate practices?

National: e.g. the scheme's contribution to poverty reduction and employment, empowering marginalised groups, improving tax revenue and export earnings, improving technology, and other issues regarding the purpose and contribution of the scheme to sustainable development. A key question: is the scheme contributing to national visions and plans for sustainable development?

Global: e.g. improving equity in development between countries, and issues concerning global public services, such as protection of globally significant biodiversity and managing the balance of greenhouse gases. A key question: does the scheme reflect international norms and obligations on human rights, environmental and economic development?

It is important not to make the mistake of treating sustainable development as 'implementing the best global principles'. It is best to build on locally agreed approaches, introducing international precepts only to deal with global issues (above) or to serve as guidance on how to fill gaps at any level.

policies are both coherent with each other and informed by the CDM rules.

Identify priorities and opportunities for projects

Prospective investors, host country institutions or local NGOs may all be involved in identifying opportunities for CDM projects. This is likely to become an on-going process informed by national priorities and strategies for land use and by improved understanding of the carbon flows in the rural sector. It is worth noting that potential investors in CDM project development and host country institutions are likely to have rather different perspectives on potential projects. For investors, the priority will be to identify projects that give a good return with manageable risk. For host countries, the objective will likely be to achieve wider development objectives by making effective use of their carbon assets.

Examples of the practical questions that local stakeholders and host country institutions should ask are:

- What scale and type of afforestation will best fit with the pattern of local farming?
- Will land tied up in forestry affect an area's food security?
- Where might afforestation reduce water availability?
- How will forestry schemes affect the demand for labour at certain times?
- Which types of investment could improve local skills and capacities?
- Will management for increased carbon storage reduce income from timber?

Promote investment into land-use CDM projects

Realisation of CDM benefits will depend on successful sales of carbon credits and attraction of foreign investors. The following activities, with government leadership, can foster CDM investment to meet a country's priorities:

- Identify promising project types, assessing their potential in terms of carbon flows and associated social, economic and environmental impacts;
- Develop baselines for these project types, which can be used by project developers in the future;
- Establish the rules and conditions for investment into the project types selected;
- Establish the requirements for development of CDM projects, including sustainable development objectives;
- Link conditions for CDM investments with the country's regulations and incentives for foreign direct investment and trading;
- Prepare a CDM programme, or investment plan, containing all or some of the points above;
- Establish a clear focal point for foreign investors to find out about CDM opportunities;
- Offer information about CDM opportunities in the country, through participation in trade fairs, exhibitions, and websites of national institutions.

Build capacity and infrastructure for project implementation

Infrastructure and capacity for project implementation should be in place for projects to be practicable and cost-effective. In the case of the land-use sector this may include local NGOs, credit agencies, research institutes, nurseries, technical foresters, extension officers or land-use experts. The strength of such capacity may be important in selecting priority activities and geographical areas for project development. In many cases capacity may not be adequate, but could be built up in preparation for the CDM. International funding mechanisms will be available for capacity building alongside the CDM.

Develop in-country understanding of carbon flows and data availability in the land-use sector

While projects should be based on national and local development priorities, host country institutions should also develop a good understanding of the carbon flows under different land uses, so that they can determine the technical potential of various CDM options. While there is no specific requirement within the Kyoto Protocol for CDM project data to be cross-referenced to national emissions data, some link between them will help to improve the quality of both project and national scale datasets.

Define the legal landscape for carbon ownership

A key issue for the security of carbon credits generated from any project is the question of who owns the emission reduction. National laws regarding property ownership may need to be reviewed to determine how project developers can make an unencumbered claim to ownership. In cases where land, crops and trees are owned by a single individual or company this may be relatively simple to demonstrate. However, in situations where such rights are separated, as on national, communal or tenanted land, or where certain groups have customary or statutory rights of access, there may be various legal complexities to resolve.

What forest and land-use principles should be used to design and screen CDM projects?

The *purpose* of a CDM project should be consistent with agreed national visions, strategies, plans and targets for sustainable development. Two types of initiative can be used to ensure this: criteria or standards for sustainable land management at project level; and sustainable development plans at national level.

At the **project level**, existing sets of sustainability criteria, indicators and standards can be helpful to judge sustainability. As far as possible, they should also reflect sustainable development agreements at the national and global level. Most criteria and indicators (C&I) of good forest management have a degree of international compatibility (such as those of the International Tropical Timber Organisation[1]), although as yet there is no set of criteria that is globally accepted.

The non-governmental Forest Stewardship Council[2] (FSC) maintains a global set of ten principles and associated criteria for good forest management, covering social, environmental and economic factors. These are to be specified in terms of national standards by multi-stakeholder national working groups, and interpreted by forest managers and certifiers alike for local conditions. In contrast to forestry, there are limited criteria and indicators for sustainable land use and agriculture, especially for complex mixed systems including agroforestry. However, the International Federation of Organic Agriculture Movements[3] (IFOAM) sets a basic international standard for organic agriculture and accreditation criteria for organic certification programmes. Individual countries may also have regulations and guidelines that should be employed. For biodiversity, indicators are currently being developed by the Convention on Biodiversity.

Useful procedures for assessing sustainability at project level include: environmental and social impact assessment and forest certification, both of which may be employed before and during the project. Environmental and social impact assessment procedures should operate according to national legal standards, be recognised as valuable by national stakeholders, be transparent, and enable clear mitigation options to emerge.

At the **national level** the challenge is to ascertain which existing sustainable development plans and strategies can offer useful guidance as to what kinds of CDM project will be desirable. The most useful national initiatives will be those that are actively applied and are meaningful locally. Six important types are described below. However, experience with sustainable development is relatively new, and many initiatives will not provide the full guidance a CDM project is seeking. (There is little point in screening a CDM project according to an initiative that meets with local disapproval, or is an unrealistic dream.) Assessing the national initiatives against the following criteria[4] may be helpful to assess which one(s) to use,

---

1 *www.itto.or.jp*
2 *www.fscoax.org*
3 *www.ifoam.org*
4 *Summarised from current UN-DESA (2002) and OECD Development Assistance Committee (2001) guidance on national strategies for sustainable development.*

both to develop national strategies for CDM, and to develop and screen an individual CDM project. National strategies should:

- have a balanced coverage of environmental, social, and economic dimensions;
- be formulated with participatory, multi-stakeholder input that involves government, civil society and business sectors;
- seek out and respond to local needs;
- be linked to international initiatives, e.g. the environmental conventions;
- have high-level political and legal backing;
- be characterised by continuous systems, and not just by a 'wish-list';
- be actively implemented and monitored.

One or more of the following initiatives may provide guidance on the development of national strategies for CDM and may help design and/or screen individual projects:

1. The *'National Forest Programme'* (NFP) offers specificity on desirable forestry practices and investment in forestry. It is supposed to be an articulation of (a rather unwieldy) 270 internationally agreed 'proposals for action'. The more recent NFPs meet many of the above criteria. The NFP is also likely to be consistent with the set of forestry C&I that is agreed as applying to forest management in the country.
2. *The various national action plans for international environmental conventions* – notably on biodiversity and desertification – offer some specificity on what environmental objectives are expected to be mainstreamed and what indicators to look for, and they call for Environmental Impact Assessments of projects such as CDM.
3. *'Poverty reduction strategies'*[5] offer specificity on what is considered desirable in terms of improving livelihoods, and can help to make social objectives clearer. However, some may be more an expression of donor intention than national commitment; and they may have an incomplete consideration of environmental issues.
4. *'Local Agenda 21s'* offer specificity on local priorities for integrating social, environmental and economic objectives. They take the form of a plan for sustainable development for a given district, which should show the broad kinds of land use that are considered desirable.
5. *Land-use plans* may be of many types, but government-organised plans are often the preserve of technocrats. As such, they may provide little guidance on local sustainability requirements other than information on land capability and suitability. Although government

5 *www.worldbank.org/poverty/strategies*

land use planning is often in disarray in many developing countries (and is consequently ignored), some rural development projects are 'reinventing' it through more participatory approaches. Especially where these are based on large-scale common property resource systems, they have potential for helping the rural poor meet the scale requirements of CDM projects.

6. *'National strategies for sustainable development (nssds)'*[6] are currently being developed to sort out the multiple trade-offs for sustainable development in ways that meet the above criteria. The concept of *nssds* was agreed in 1992 at Rio as a way to organise 'Agenda 21' at the national level through government, civil society and business partnerships. Only recently has there been guidance on *nssds*, from the United Nations and OECD. However, not many *nssds* exist as yet, or meet all the above criteria.

6 *www.nssd.net*

3. How are **CDM** projects developed?

Irrespective of whether CDM projects are initiated by the private sector, non-government organisations or government agencies, their development will involve a number of essential steps. This section outlines these requirements, from a project developer's perspective. They are illustrated in the diagram below. The shading in the diagram represents the group responsible for the activity: project developer, host government, operational entity (third party certifier), or CDM Executive Board.

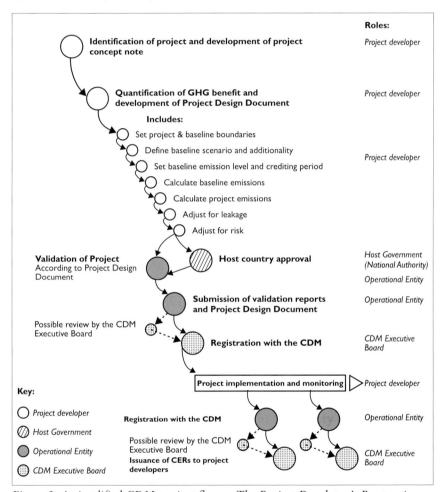

Figure 3: A simplified CDM project flow – The Project Developer's Perspective

Identify project and develop project concept note

The first stage is the identification of the potential CDM project. This will need to take into account any national or regional requirements for project eligibility. Project developers should note that potential investors and verification bodies will also operate their own screening procedures. It is important that local stakeholders' needs and aspirations are considered at this early stage.

Quantify greenhouse gas benefits

Each project plan should include details of how the greenhouse gas benefits are calculated and how they will be monitored over time. In most cases the quantification of benefits will begin prior to submission to the National CDM Authority. Quantification involves the following steps:

- *Definition of the boundaries of the project* – this will result in a list of all the processes that result in uptake or release of carbon (and other greenhouse gases covered by the Kyoto Protocol) as a result of the project activities.
- *Description of the baseline and additionality* – the effect of the project is measured relative to a 'baseline scenario' that represents what would happen in the absence of the project. Additionality is the extent to which the activities promoted by the project (e.g. the planting of trees) can only have happened with the project's specific intervention. The precise interpretation of additionality and the methods used to measure it are among the details still under discussion between the parties to the Climate Change Convention.
- *Quantification of baseline emissions and crediting period* – the emissions that would occur with the baseline scenario, and the number of years over which the project may take credit, will be defined using one of the procedures approved by the CDM Executive Board.
- *The emissions and uptake of carbon by the project* – in the case of afforestation and reforestation projects, the uptake of carbon will be calculated using forestry growth data. The net benefit of the project is then calculated by subtracting the emissions that would have occurred in the baseline scenario.
- *Adjustment for leakage and risk* – The amount of benefit for which a project will be allowed to take credit may need to be adjusted to take account of leakage and risks. The specific procedures to be applied are still being decided by the CDM Executive Board, but creating a reserve or buffer of carbon offsets is one method that has been proposed for dealing with project risks. The best approach to managing leakage is to avoid it in the first place. This is best done at the project design stage, notably by:
  - Consultation with local stakeholders;
  - Integration of project design with local, regional and/or national priorities and legislation;
  - Participation of landowners or managers in the project, avoiding their exclusion or displacement;
  - Clear and fair benefit sharing through the project;

  – Awareness building of carbon project needs;
  – Effective monitoring of project activities and likely sources of leakage.

Since the procedures for quantifying the greenhouse gas benefits of individual projects are rather complex and onerous, project developers and/or host country institutions may wish to consider grouping small-scale projects, so that the costs of technical work and the risks can be spread. Plan Vivo[7] uses a management system that can be used to aggregate the benefits from many similar small-scale forestry activities (see Box 6).

Develop a Project Design Document
The results and methodologies used in the quantification of the greenhouse gas benefits will need to be presented in a Project Design Document. A report summarising comments by local stakeholders and how these are taken into account in the project design must also be included in this document.

Host country approval
Any project wishing to participate in the CDM must obtain approval from the host government. A pro-active government National Authority for CDM will facilitate this. In addition, the host government should determine whether or not the project will lead to sustainable development benefits.

Validation of the project
Before projects can produce emission reductions that will be recognised by the CDM, they must be 'validated' by one of the independent companies approved by the CDM Executive Board. The project developer must submit the Project Design Document and any related documentation to the so-called 'operational entity'. The process will involve detailed scrutiny of the institutional capacity of the project stakeholders, the evidence underlying the calculations of carbon benefits, the systems to be used for monitoring, and of course the relevant government approvals. During this period, the Project Design Document will be made publicly available for comments.

Registration with the CDM
The validation report and Project Design Document will be submitted to the CDM Executive Board by the operational entity. Registration will be finalised after a maximum of eight weeks from receipt, unless a review is requested.

7 *www.planvivo.org*

Box 6: Scolel Té and the Plan Vivo system

In 1994 a group of researchers from the University of Edinburgh and El Colegio de la Frontera Sur in Mexico, undertook a study to ascertain whether sales of carbon services could improve rural livelihoods among indigenous farmers in Chiapas, southern Mexico. The study identified the need for a flexible but structured administrative framework to aggregate the carbon benefits from many small-scale activities. Individual farmers wanted the right to choose how and when to participate, and it was assumed that purchasers and regulatory authorities would require effective monitoring and verification procedures.

Over the next 3 years, funding from UK DFID's Forestry Research Programme was used to develop an integrated planning, administration and monitoring system, based upon the requirements identified in the study. The system became known as Plan Vivo. In 1997, the collaborating organisations secured the interest of a purchaser of carbon services. The pilot project, known as Scolel Té ('the tree that grows') began with an agreement to provide 18,000 tCO_2 'prototype carbon credits' per year, at a price of US\$ 2.7 per tCO_2 (US\$10 per tC) to the International Automobile Federation. These funds were used to provide farmers with carbon payments to cover the costs of establishing agroforestry systems, small-scale plantations and communal reforestation activities.

The Scolel Té project is now run by a trust fund – the Fondo BioClimatico – which has become a financially viable organisation, whose income is derived from the sale of carbon services. There are currently over 400 individual participants from about 30 communities, representing four different ethnic groups and a wide range of agro-ecosystems.

The Plan Vivo system is now also being used in an agroforestry and bioenergy project in southern India, run by an NGO called 'Women for Sustainable Development'. There are plans for further projects in Mozambique and Uganda. Current development involves the international verification company, SGS, and organizations in Mexico and India in efforts to ensure the system's compatibility with the requirements for CDM.

Project implementation and monitoring

Registered projects, and those that have entered the implementation phase, will be required to maintain internal monitoring systems to demonstrate they are achieving the emission reductions specified in the Project Design Document.

Verification and certification

Once the project is being implemented, it will undergo additional scrutiny by the operational entities in the form of verification and certification. The verification report is then made available to the CDM Executive Board and the general public, after which the Certified Emission Reductions will be issued to the project developer within 15 days, unless the Executive Board requests a review.

4. What can we expect as the CDM evolves?

Will the benefits of the CDM be worth our effort?

The uptake, storage and release of carbon by terrestrial vegetation look likely to have increasing economic implications over the coming decades. The institutions responsible for land use will therefore need to begin to integrate carbon considerations into the other objectives of land management.

Certain questions should be kept under review as the CDM market develops, to better ascertain whether or not to encourage CDM projects in the land-use sector – notably: who could benefit? by how much? under what conditions? can other funds and benefits be leveraged? The CDM may not always be the best mechanism for a land-use project or for securing social, economic and environmental improvement. As climate change awareness increases worldwide, parallel programs promoting carbon sequestration are likely to be promoted, as in the case of carbon-funded forest conservation programmes promoted by some environmental NGOs.

What impacts can we expect on land use in developing countries?

The impacts that the CDM will have on land use will largely depend on details yet to be decided and adopted by the CDM Executive Board – on project eligibility, the conditions required to ensure the permanence of project benefits, and procedures to set baselines. Purchasers of carbon currently favour projects in the energy and industrial sectors, partly as a result of the continued uncertainty on eligibility, but also due to the perceived risks associated with land-use projects.

In the land-use sector, an emphasis on forestry projects – as opposed to agricultural activities – will continue, primarily because of: the relatively high rate of carbon uptake and ease of measurement of carbon in trees relative to soils; the short (five–year) commitment periods for emission reductions; and the readier availability of forestry criteria and standards that are accepted at global level as well as locally.

Unless there is some active intervention on the part of developing country governments and agencies wishing to promote people-oriented forestry, an emphasis on simple forest types, notably single-species plantations, in unpopulated areas with few 'people' issues may emerge. This is simpler to organise than smaller-scale, livelihood-oriented, complex forestry (which, despite its local benefits, tends not to be recognised by current forestry standards).

An emphasis on large-scale forestry schemes may also emerge, on land with good growth rates, using technologies to improve those rates. The financial profit margins on almost all land-use activities are slight – and so the trend is for bigger operations that gain benefits from economies of scale. The transaction costs involved in a CDM project are also significant: there are considerable information, negotiation, design, monitoring and risk management requirements. Only big operations will be able to meet such requirements, unless there is some intervention to aggregate or share costs between many smaller projects.

Such large-scale, simple forestry projects that avoid (or evade) 'people' issues can be very effective at delivering carbon storage. But they run the risk of running counter to other sustainable development initiatives that seek multiple goods and services from forests, and that seek to return power and beneficial rights to poor and forest-dependent people. Hence the need to ensure that CDM projects are informed by, and supportive of, locally-accepted sustainable development initiatives.

What impacts can we expect on livelihoods, especially for the poor?

Where forest goods and services are scarce, technologies and investment are lacking, or employment opportunities are few, CDM land-use projects could benefit communities – especially if there are agreements to ensure access to these benefits by needy parts of the community. But such projects can also have negative impacts on local food security and development options. It is too easy for governments and corporations to assume that 'empty' land is not being used.

Given a likely emphasis on large-scale forestry, whether livelihoods improve depends on:

- Who runs the projects, and
- How those projects are implemented.

The requirements of the CDM 'project flow' can be daunting for smaller groups with few international connections. The transaction costs can be high. Thus it will be more difficult for smaller companies and community groups to access the benefits of CDM. The livelihood impacts of projects run by large companies will consequently tend to be determined by: the social standards selected (one reason to get the sustainable development criteria right); their application in practice (a reason to link up with active sustainable development initiatives that can ensure that afforestation does not take place on land which is socially important); and by the scope for corporate-community partnerships.

If smallholders/communities are to be actively involved in a CDM project, not only must their land-use systems be recognised by the sustainable development criteria applied to CDM nationally, but also the transaction costs must be overcome. This can be done if a third party (e.g. NGO, rural development bank or government extension service) brings people together into a group scheme, assuring the provision of information, the consistency of the management regime, and the financial and administration systems for cost-benefit sharing amongst many small players. The sustainable livelihoods framework can be a useful diagnostic when assessing the impacts of such group projects.[8]

Ultimately, carbon conservation activities (management of natural forests for biodiversity, ecotourism, watershed and other non-consumptive activities) may offer some of the highest livelihood benefits rather than afforestation. However, these are not yet eligible under the CDM. Of the eligible activities, agroforestry and integrated rural forestry and energy projects have considerable livelihood benefits.

What corporate behaviour can we expect from CDM investors?

Private sector enterprises will play a key role in implementing the CDM. Companies will both develop project ideas and invest in approved schemes (see Box 7). Companies are also likely to get involved in CDM activities where they already have operations in the host country. Projects are likely to be selected primarily on considerations of financial returns and on alignment with existing business activities. For this reason, forestry activities may be relatively unpopular.

In mainstream commercial forestry, the evidence of long-term commercial benefits from adopting high environmental and social standards is patchy. For conservative investors, this is likely to constrain take-up of those CDM opportunities that are only marginally economically viable. In contrast, a few more innovative companies may see potential gains, in terms of corporate reputation, by investing in socially responsible forestry projects.

---

8 *www.livelihoods.org*

> ## Box 7: Large scale plantation forestry in Tanzania
>
> Tree Farms AS, a Norwegian forestry company, hopes to sell carbon credits to private GHG emitters in Norway as the Kyoto Protocol targets begin to bite and the government presses companies to attain emission reductions. Currently only one utility company, Industrikraft Midt-Norge, has indicated plans to purchase forest-based offsets under the CDM. In 1996, it agreed to a provisional carbon offset options contract (which gives it the option to purchase carbon offsets at a designated future date at a price agreed today) with Tree Farms AS at just under US\$ 4.5/tCO$_2$. The options would be exercised during the first Kyoto commitment period 2008–2012.
>
> Carbon offsets are to be supplied through afforestation using eucalyptus and pine in East Africa. In Tanzania three sites are being leased in the highlands, totalling 87,568 hectares, with afforestation by a Tree Farms subsidiary. Because leases, which last for 99 years, can be obtained only through a complex and bureaucratic application process involving approval from community organisations through to ministerial agencies, the company is still awaiting final approval. Nevertheless, planting has started (approximately 1,840 hectares in 2000) and the company is aiming to produce carbon offsets alongside timber. Estimated carbon revenues over a 25-year period come to \$27 million from just one of its three plantations.

In this context, developing countries need to define the sustainable development criteria and the corporate codes of conduct that should be applicable in their countries.

Where will investment go and what do developing countries need to do?

As the global CDM market evolves, it is likely to follow the path of much of foreign direct investment over the past decades. The bulk may go to a dozen or so larger developing countries with the infrastructure and institutions to handle large projects easily. For the vast majority of the poorer developing countries, the private sector, left to itself, is unlikely to pay very much attention unless steps are actively taken to attract CDM projects. This could be done in two ways:

- Using portfolio investors such as the Prototype Carbon Fund of the World Bank and other large financial institutions, who may wish to spread their projects around the developing world especially in poorer developing countries, where the private sector on its own would not invest;
- Using international development assistance funds to help poorer developing countries to build the national capacity to develop and promote CDM projects.

How will the global CDM market develop?

The future of the global market will depend largely on the demand for CDM projects from companies and countries in the north. Without the USA participating in the Kyoto CDM market (although it may set up a parallel market on its own), the demand is likely to be substantially constrained, reducing capital available for the development of these projects.

Furthermore, developing countries that are looking to the CDM market to promote both inward investments and sustainable development projects, will judge the market not just by how many CDM projects it is able to generate but also by how many countries have been able to benefit. If only a few developing countries benefit, then it may be difficult for the rest of the developing countries to agree to further extensions of the CDM concept in future commitment periods.

5. Where can I get more information?

There is a wealth of information available on the CDM. Finding the right information is not always easy. A cross-section of websites and information sources is provided below, with a particular preference for those that contain good links to other sources. This list is by no means exhaustive, and its inclusion does not necessarily imply endorsement by the authors.

Where do I find out about official meetings and texts?

United Nations Framework Convention on Climate Change (UNFCCC) – http://www.unfccc.int – The UNFCCC keeps a complete list of documents relating to the convention on its website including the Kyoto Protocol as well as access to Country Reports. It includes all reports on COPs. Access the documentation by clicking the 'Resources' button.

UNFCCC–CDM site – http://unfccc.int/cdm/ – For information on the CDM, meetings of the Executive Board and the project activity cycle.

National Communications Support Programme – http://www.undp.org/gef/cc/ – The National Communications Support Programme works with more than 130 participating countries in eight sub-regions: Africa, Arab States, Europe and the CIS, Asia, the Pacific, the Caribbean, and Central and South America. It was launched by the UNDP and the UNEP, in co-operation with the Secretariat of the UNFCCC. The Programme provides technical support to enhance the capacity of non-Annex I parties to prepare their initial National Communications. It also aims to promote the quality, comprehensiveness, and timeliness of initial National Communications.

IPCC Special Report on Land Use, Land-use Change and Forestry (LULUCF) – http://www.ipcc.ch/. All IPCC Special Reports can be downloaded as well as other publications and information on the work of the IPCC.

Where would I find out more about the climate policy process?

International Institute for Sustainable Development (IISD), Canada – http://iisd1.iisd.ca/climatechange.htm – Publishes an electronic newsletter on all important international meetings on climate change (including COPs).

Pew Centre for Climate Change – http://www.pewclimate.org/ – Publishes articles on climate change related issues aimed at US corporations and public.

Earth Negotiations Bulletin (ENB) – http://www.iisd.ca/linkages/climate/ – Provides daily coverage on the COP meetings, including an analysis of the negotiations and reports of side events.

Climate Policy – http://www.climatepolicy.com – A research journal looking at national and international policy response to climate change, including forestry and the CDM.

Centre for Clean Air Policy (CCAP) – http://www.ccap.org/ – Provides up to date news, papers and discussions on domestic and international climate change policies, including the role of land use in the CDM.

Resources for the Future (RFF) – http://www.rff.org/ – Draws on an extensive 'think tank' of expert researchers, focusing primarily on the economic and social sciences in natural resource issues. The site has an extensive on-line library with separate sections on forestry, land use and climate.

How can I find out about the science and research surrounding the CDM?

IPCC Data Distribution Centre (DDC) – http://ipcc-ddc.cru.uea.ac.uk/ – Established to facilitate the timely distribution of a consistent set of up-to-date scenarios of changes in climate and related environmental and socio-economic factors for use in climate impacts assessments. The intention is that these new assessments can feed into the review process of the IPCC, in particular to the Third Assessment Report (TAR).

IPCC National Greenhouse Gas Inventories Programme – http://www.ipcc-nggip.iges.or.jp/

Pacific Institute for Studies in Development – http://www.pacinst.org/ – An independent, non-profit centre created in 1987 to conduct research and policy analysis in environment, sustainable development, and international security, with a focus on long-term solutions that require an interdisciplinary perspective.

Bangladesh Centre for Advanced Studies (BCAS), Bangladesh – http://www.bcas.net – Has a number of publications mainly on vulnerability and impacts of climate change in Bangladesh

Center for International Forestry Research (CIFOR) –
http://www.cifor.cgiar.org/ – Covers the sustainable management and use
of forests in developing countries, particularly the tropics. This includes
work on forest carbon, sustainable livelihoods and biodiversity.

The FAO Climate change and forestry mailing list –
http://www.fao.org/forestry/climate – Regular email updates on all issues
relating to climate change and forestry, including publications, policy
news, projects, and interesting websites.

International Institute for Environment and Development (IIED) –
http://www.iied.org/ – An independent, non-profit organization promoting
sustainable patterns of world development through collaborative research,
policy studies, networking and knowledge dissemination. The site includes
information on sustainable development criteria and strategies, forestry,
land use and climate change, with a large list of publications that can be
downloaded.

Forest Trends – http://www.forest-trends.org/ – An organisation that aims
to promote market-based approaches to forest conservation. Their website
has some good links to other information sources on forestry issues,
including a section on forest carbon under 'forest services'.

Climate Ark (climate change and renewable energy portal) –
http://www.climateark.org/ – An internet portal dedicated to promoting
public policy that addresses global climate change through reductions in
carbon dioxide and other emissions, renewable energy, energy
conservation and ending deforestation. Climate Ark provides a useful
search engine on climate change-related issues, and links to current and
past news.

Where can I find out more about pilot carbon projects?
Activities Implemented Jointly (AIJ) –
http://unfccc.int/program/aij/aijproj.html – The UNFCCC's official list of
AIJ projects accepted by the designated national authorities.

ICRAF (International Centre for Research in Agroforestry) –
http://www.icraf.cgiar.org – ICRAF, based in Nairobi, Kenya, maintains
information on agroforestry activities including some pilot CDM projects.

Face Foundation – http://www.facefoundation.nl/- FACE (Forests
Absorbing Carbon dioxide Emissions) is a non-profit organisation that has
been funding the planting and maintenance of forests since 1990.

Ilha do Bananal – http://www.ecologica.org.br – a pilot carbon offset and conservation project in Brazil.

South-south north – http://www.southsouthnorth.org/ – The mission of the SouthSouthNorth Project, or SSN Project, is to design, develop and implement Clean Development Mechanism projects under the Kyoto Protocol

Plan Vivo – http://www.planvivo.org/ – The site holds an online manual for the Plan Vivo Systems for planning, managing and monitoring the supply of carbon services from small farmers, particularly in developing countries, in ways that enhance rural livelihoods.

The Nature Conservancy (TNC) – http://nature.org/aboutus/projects/climate/ – TNC is a conservation organisation in the USA, with partner organisations in Asia-Pacific, Canada, the Caribbean and Latin America, working to preserve plants animals and natural communities, mainly through land purchases. It is involved in climate change projects in several counties including Rio Bravo in Belize and Noel Kempff in Bolivia.

The Center for Environmental Leadership in Business, at Conservation International – http://www.celb.org – Builds partnerships between the private sector and the environmental community, including projects to offset emissions through forest conservation and reforestation.

The World Land Trust – http://www.worldlandtrust.org – The World Land Trust is a conservation charity that purchases land in developing countries to conserve biodiversity and threatened ecosystems. It is developing policy advice for the DFID on CDM projects.

Tanzania International Small Group and Tree-planting Program (TIST) – http://www.tist.org – Formed in 1999, this is a community-driven programme to sequester carbon and create carbon storage in a way that is consistent with the best practices of sustainable development. It is developing within the context of CDM principles.

World Resources Institute (WRI) – http://www.wri.org – Information on a range of issues of importance to the CDM and land-use sectors, including some pilot CDM projects. Plenty of papers and publications are available.

United States Initiative on Joint Implementation (USIJI) – http://www.gcrio.org/usiji/ – USIJI is a pilot programme encouraging projects that mitigate greenhouse gas emissions and promote sustainable development. The site provides useful information on project development, ongoing projects, links and related documents on climate change.

Moving Towards Emissions Neutral Development (MEND) – http://www.cdmcapacity.com/MEND – was a DFID funded project to investigate how CDM projects can be implemented to optimise sustainable development targets. The focus countries were Ghana, Bangladesh, Columbia and Sri Lanka.

Carbon Monitor – a newsletter published by Environmental Intermediaries & Trading Group Limited. It covers many issues on commercialising the carbon offsets created by Kyoto and provides regular updates with commentary. You can sign up for the newsletter free by emailing Richard Hayes – rhayes@nznet.gen.nz

Where can I go for institutional support?

US Country Studies Program – http://www.gcrio.org/CSP/webpage.html – Through the U.S. Country Studies Program, the US Government has been providing technical and financial support to 56 developing countries and countries with economies in transition to assist them in conducting climate change studies. The studies have enabled these countries to develop inventories of their anthropogenic emissions of greenhouse gases, assess their vulnerabilities to climate change, and evaluate response strategies for mitigating and adapting to climate change. The program was announced by the President prior to the United Nations Conference on Environment and Development (UNCED), also known as the Earth Summit, in Rio de Janeiro, Brazil, in 1992.

The Global Environment Facility (GEF) – www.gefweb.org – The GEF is funded by the World Bank and works in conjunction with national governments, NGOs and scientific organisations to provide grants for projects on biodiversity, climate change, international waters and ozone. Projects funded include carbon sink protection, enhancement and restoration projects that improve carbon storage in biomass and soils.

The Joint Implementation Network (JIN), the Netherlands – http://www.northsea.nl/jiq – was created in 1994 to establish an international network for research and information exchange about JI, including CDM mechanisms and projects. It publishes the Joint Implementation Quarterly which reviews current developments and project progress.

How can I find out more about selling credits or getting financial assistance?

The Prototype Carbon Fund (PCF) – http://www.prototypecarbonfund.org/ – The World Bank's PCF aims to demonstrate how project-based emissions transactions can mitigate climate change. The site contains news items, discussion arenas, and key documents on projects that have applied to the PCF, including baseline studies, monitoring and verification protocols and purchase agreements.

CERUPT – http://www.senter.nl/asp/page.asp?id=i001236&alias=erupt – Funded by the Dutch government, the CERUPT programme purchases carbon credits from CDM projects. The programme is run by Senter, the agency responsible for the execution of grant schemes on behalf of a range of Dutch ministries. To date, CERUPT has not accepted credits from land-use CDM projects.

Future Forests – http://www.futureforests.com – A UK company offering voluntary carbon offsets to companies and individuals. It purchases carbon credits from forestry projects in the UK and in developing countries.

PrimaKlima – http://www.primaklima-weltweit.de – A German organisation which finances and implements afforestation, forest management and forest conservation projects in cooperation with nationally and internationally recognised organisations in order to mitigate global climate change. It is also carrying out research on behalf of the EC on guidelines for JI/CDM projects.

EcoSecurities Ltd – http://www.ecosecurities.com/100services/130financial_services.html – An environmental finance services advisory firm that provides technical, policy and financial advice on climate change issues, with specialisations in land use and the CDM.

Where can I go for help and advice?

Environment and Development Action in the Third World (ENDA) – http://www.enda.sn/ – Although primarily with a focus on energy, ENDA has an active climate change group and provides an insight into the opportunities for the CDM, especially in Africa.

Tata Energy Research Institute (TERI), India – http://www.teriin.org – Has a large number of items on climate change issues, including CDM in India. Also publishes a regular newsletter.

The Edinburgh Centre for Carbon Management (ECCM) –
http://www.eccm.uk.com – ECCM provides policy and technical advice to
government and industry in the areas of forestry and land use. ECCM also
develops carbon sequestration projects in developing countries.

EcoSecurities Ltd – http://www.ecosecurities.com – The website has more
than 50 publications covering a range of issues specific to the CDM and
land-use sector including leakage, permanence, baselines, monitoring and
crediting.

Winrock International – http://www.winrock.org/ – Employs a group of
experts in quantification and monitoring of carbon in large projects, as
well as technical support services for agriculture, forestry and natural
resources management.

**Oak Ridge National Laboratory (ORNL) Carbon Dioxide Information
Analysis Center (CDIAC)** – http://cdiac.esd.ornl.gov – the primary global-
change data and information analysis centre of the US Department of
Energy (DOE). It has large data holdings relevant to many areas of climate
change.

Trexler and Associates, Inc. (TAA) – www.climateservices.com – Trexler
provides climate change risk management services to large companies and
develops mitigation projects including forestry offset projects.

Société Generale de Surveillance (SGS) –
http://www.sgs.nl/agro/pages/carbonoffset.asp – SGS already has
experience with the certification of a number of land-use projects and
executive summaries are available on the website.

Glossary: Terms related to Carbon Credits:

Since the early 1990s, a variety of terms have been used in project-level climate change mitigation mechanisms and their outputs. The meanings of many terms have evolved in this period. Below are some of the definitions that have been used. Most terms bear some relation to the requirements of the UN Framework Convention on Climate Change (UNFCCC) signed in 1992, whose provisions are fleshed out by the Kyoto Protocol, signed in December 1997.

Mechanisms (1) – early pre-Kyoto definitions

Joint Implementation (JI)
The concept of Joint Implementation (JI) was introduced by Norway into pre-UNCED negotiations in 1991. This was reflected in Article 4.2(a) of the UNFCCC which gives Annex I countries (see below) the option of contributing to the Convention's objectives by implementing policies and measures jointly with other countries. The investing participants in these projects expected to claim emission reduction 'credits' for the activities financed, which would lower their greenhouse gas (GHG) liabilities (eg carbon taxes, emission caps) in their home countries. This expectation has not been realised.

Activities Implemented Jointly (AIJ)
In the first Conference of the Parties (CoP 1) to the UNFCCC held in 1995 in Berlin, developing country dissatisfaction with the JI model was voiced as a formal refusal of JI with crediting against objectives set by the Convention (see text for full discussion). Instead, a compromise was found in the form of a pilot phase, during which projects were called Activities Implemented Jointly (AIJ). During the AIJ Pilot Phase, projects were conducted with the objective of establishing protocols and experiences, but without allowing carbon credits to be transferred between developed and developing countries. It was decided at CoP 6 Part II in Bonn to continue the AIJ Pilot Phase.

Mechanisms (2) – post-Kyoto definitions
The Kyoto Protocol of the UNFCCC created three instruments, collectively known as the 'flexibility mechanisms', to facilitate accomplishment of the objectives of the Convention. A new terminology was adopted to refer to these mechanisms, as detailed below. Note that because of the Kyoto Protocol's distinction between projects carried out in the developed and developing world, some AIJ projects may be reclassified as CDM or JI projects.

Joint Implementation (JI)

Set out in Article 6 of the Protocol, JI refers to climate change mitigation projects implemented between two Annex 1 countries (see below). JI allows for the creation, acquisition and transfer of 'emission reduction units' or ERUs.

The Clean Development Mechanism (CDM)

The CDM was established by Article 12 of the Protocol and refers to climate change mitigation projects undertaken between Annex 1 countries and non-Annex 1 countries (see below). This new mechanism, whilst resembling JI, has important points of difference. In particular, project investments must contribute to the sustainable development of the non-Annex 1 host country, and must also be independently certified. This latter requirement gives rise to the term 'certified emissions reductions' or CERs, which describe the output of CDM projects, and which under the terms of Article 12 can be banked from the year 2000, eight years before the first commitment period (2008–2012).

Emissions Trading (ET)

Article 17 of the Protocol allows for emissions-capped Annex B countries (see below) to transfer among themselves portions of their assigned amounts (AAs) of GHG emissions. Under this mechanism, countries that emit less than they are allowed under the Protocol (their AAs) can sell surplus allowances to those countries that have surpassed their AAs. Such transfers do not necessarily have to be directly linked to emission reductions from specific projects.

Which countries are in which mechanisms?

Annex 1 countries

These are the 36 industrialised countries and economies in transition listed in Annex 1 of the UNFCCC. Their responsibilities under the Convention are various, and include a non-binding commitment to reducing their GHG emissions to 1990 levels by the year 2000.

Annex B countries

These are the 39 emissions-capped industrialised countries and economies in transition listed in Annex B of the Kyoto Protocol. Legally-binding emission reduction obligations for Annex B countries range from an 8 percent decrease (eg EC) to a 10 percent increase (Iceland) on 1990 levels by the first commitment period of the Protocol, 2008–2012.

Annex I or Annex B?

In practice, Annex 1 of the Convention and Annex B of the Protocol are used almost interchangeably. However, strictly speaking, it is the Annex 1 countries that can invest in JI/CDM projects as well as host JI projects, and non-Annex 1 countries that can host CDM projects, even though it is the Annex B countries that have the emission reduction obligations under the Protocol. Note that Belorus and Turkey are listed in Annex 1 but not Annex B; and that Croatia, Liechtenstein, Monaco and Slovenia are listed in Annex B but not Annex 1.

Project outputs

Carbon offsets – used in a variety of contexts, most commonly either to mean the output of carbon sequestration projects in the forestry sector, or to refer to the output of any climate change mitigation project more generally.

Carbon credits – as for carbon offsets, though with added connotations of (1) being used as 'credits' in companies' or countries' emission accounts to counter 'debits', ie emissions, and (2) being tradable, or at least fungible with the emission permit trading system.

ERUs (emission reduction units) – the technical term for the output of JI projects, as defined by the Kyoto Protocol.

CERs (certified emission reductions) – the technical term for the output of CDM projects, as defined by the Kyoto Protocol.

RMUs (removal units) – the new technical term representing sink credits generated in Annex I countries, which can be traded through the emissions trading and JI mechanisms